The Pros and Cons of SOLAR POWER

Isabel Thomas

rosen publishing's
rosen
central

New York

Published in 2008 by The Rosen Publishing Group, Inc.
29 East 21st Street, New York, NY 10010

First Edition

Series Editor: Jennifer Schofield
Editor: Debbie Foy
Consultant: Rob Bowden
Designer: Jane Hawkins
Cover designer: Paul Cherrill
Picture Researcher: Diana Morris
Illustrator: Ian Thompson
Indexer: Sue Lightfoot

Picture Acknowledgments:
Rob Bowden/EASI-Images: 14, 33. Andrew Brown/Ecoscene: 20.
Adrian Cooper/EASI-Images: 26. Anthony Cooper/Ecoscene: 18.
Ullstein Eckel/Still Pictures: 30. Ecoscene: 41. Chinch Gryniewicz/
Ecoscene: front cover br, 11, 23, 39. Angela Hampton/Ecoscene: 6.
Roy Maconachie/EASI-Images: 36. NASA: 42. Stefano Paltera/Solar
Decathlon: 45. Ed Parker/EASI-Images: 8, 24. Roger Ressmeyer/
Corbis: 34. Otto Ronge/Corbis: front cover, 16. Quilai Shen/Panos: 29.
US Dept. of Energy/SPL: 31.

Library of Congress Cataloging-in-Publication Data

Thomas, Isabel, 1980-
  the pros and cons of Solar Power / Isabel Thomas.
     p. cm. -- (Energy debate)
  Includes index.
  ISBN-13: 978-1-4042-3741-4 (lib. bdg.)
  ISBN-10: 1-4042-3741-0 (lib. bdg.)
  1. Solar energy--Juvenile literature. I. Title.
  TJ810.3.T56 2007
  333.792'3--dc22

                              2006039142

Manufactured in China

Contents

CHAPTER 1 | Solar power and the energy debate

Every person in the world depends on energy. Heat energy cooks food and warms our homes. Chemical energy in food powers our bodies. Light and sound energy allow people to see and hear. All these forms of energy share the ability to do work —to make something happen.

Endless energy

Energy cannot be made or destroyed, but it can be changed from one form to another. The chemical energy stored in wood, for example, is changed into heat and light energy by combustion (burning). The energy industry makes billions of dollars converting energy into useful forms and supplying it to people around the world.

In demand

Electricity is the most convenient form of energy. At the flick of a switch, it powers lights, telephones, and all the labor-saving gadgets that fill people's homes, schools, and offices in more economically developed countries (MEDCs). Most of the energy used to create electricity comes from burning coal, oil, and natural gas—known as *fossil fuels*. Transportation also consumes huge amounts of fossil fuel. Almost 50 million barrels of oil are made into gas and other fuels each day.

An energy crisis?

Fossil fuels were created over millions of years from the remains of dead animals and plants. They are nonrenewable resources, and one day they will run out. Coal reserves may last for 200–300 years, but oil and gas production is expected to slow down in the middle of this century. As reserves become harder to find, supplies will quickly become too expensive to use as we do today.

Limited supply is not the only danger. When fossil fuels are burned, polluting gases are released. These are creating serious environmental problems. Fumes from vehicles and industry cause hundreds of thousands of deaths every year. On a global scale, this pollution is warming the atmosphere.

The greenhouse effect

Certain gases trap some of the Sun's heat and stop it from escaping back into space. These "greenhouse gases," such as carbon dioxide (CO_2), warm the Earth enough to make life possible. When fossil fuels are burned, extra CO_2 is released into the atmosphere, increasing the greenhouse effect. The amount of CO_2 in the atmosphere has risen by 31 percent in the last 250 years, and is causing global warming.

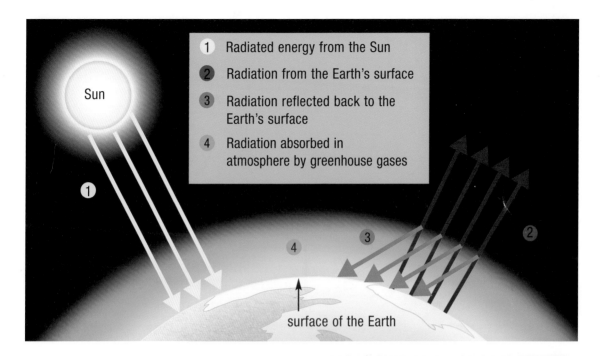

1 Radiated energy from the Sun

2 Radiation from the Earth's surface

3 Radiation reflected back to the Earth's surface

4 Radiation absorbed in atmosphere by greenhouse gases

Sun

surface of the Earth

△ An increase in the atmosphere's natural greenhouse effect is warming the Earth.

Warnings

The International Panel on Climate Change (IPCC) has warned that greenhouse gas emissions must be cut to avoid the dangerous effects of global warming, such as a rise in sea levels, severe flooding, the spread of diseases, violent weather, drought, loss of biodiversity, and food shortages.

> **We're running out of atmosphere faster than we're running out of fossil fuels. The more we diversify our sources, the better.**
>
> Dan Kammen, Head of of Renewable and Appropriate Energy Laboratory, Berkeley, California

Energy alternatives

To slow climate change, fossil fuel use must be cut down long before supplies run out. This means using less energy, and finding alternative energy sources. The energy crisis has focused attention on renewable resources. Wind, wave, water, and solar power are sustainable; they will never run out. They are also seen as "green" energies, because they do not directly produce greenhouse gases. However, every energy source has its drawbacks. The challenge is to find an energy mix that will tackle climate change and supply reliable, affordable energy into the future.

Developing solar power around the world

Scientists and inventors have experimented with alternative energy sources for centuries, but serious interest in renewables began in the 1970s. A steep rise in oil prices shocked countries that were used to cheap energy. They rushed to find ways to reduce their dependency on expensive imported oil.

Using heat and light energy from the Sun seemed an attractive solution—every hour, the Earth receives more energy from the Sun than its 6 billion people use in a year. Solar energy will not run out and it does not give off greenhouse gases. Finding a way to convert this energy into useful forms would solve our energy problems.

The Solar Energy Research Institute (now the National Renewable Energy

△ Pollution from burning fossil fuels has become a major problem, especially in big cities such as Los Angeles, California. It is prompting governments to take action.

Laboratory) was opened in 1977 to develop solar technology. In 1982, the world's first solar power plant opened in the United States. However, when the price of fossil fuels fell again in the 1980s, enthusiasm for renewable energies faded. Industry and individuals were more interested in saving money in the short-term than contemplating the long-term environmental cost.

Meanwhile, evidence for global warming continued to grow. In 1997, an agreement was drawn up in Kyoto, Japan, to commit countries to reducing greenhouse gas emissions. This was an important step toward global recognition of the problem.

In the early 2000s, Kyoto targets, the return of high oil prices, and fears about energy security have led to more investment in solar power.

Will the Kyoto agreement make a difference?

Energy use is not equal around the world. MEDCs are home to just 20 percent of the world's population, but their power plants, factories, and cars produce 80 percent of global carbon emissions. The United States alone is responsible for 22 percent of the CO_2 being released into the Earth's atmosphere by human activities. The lifestyle of the average citizen in the U.K. releases eight times more CO_2 than that of the average Indian citizen.

The "rule book" of Kyoto was finalized at the U.N. Climate Change Conference in 2005. More than 30 MEDCs agreed to reduce their carbon emissions by 2012. Some, including the U.S. and Australia, refused to sign, although they have scheduled their own environmental policies. However, rapid economic development and growth in countries such as China and India mean that world energy consumption continues to grow.

China and India are using their huge reserves of coal, the worst greenhouse gas emitter, to fuel their industries and power stations. Millions of people in these countries will soon own cars, as they catch up with MEDCs' standard of living. The International Energy Agency (IEA) predicts that global energy demand will increase by 50–60 percent by 2030. If this is generated from fossil fuels, greenhouse gas emissions will rise by 50 percent, canceling out any reductions made under agreements such as Kyoto.

The search for alternative energy sources must meet the needs of less economically developed countries (LEDCs), too. Solar power has great potential, but in 2004 it was supplying less than 0.01 percent of the world's primary energy. Is it possible to scale up solar power enough to make it a key part of the future energy mix?

"If we don't have a proactive energy policy, we'll just wind up using [dirtier fossil fuels], and it will be a continually diminishing return, and eventually our civilization will collapse. But it doesn't have to end that way. We have a choice."

Professor Emeritus Martin Hoffert, New York University, New York

CHAPTER 2 What is solar power?

△ The Sun is the energy source for all life on Earth. Green plants can convert the energy in sunlight into storable chemical energy.

Most of the energy we use originates from the Sun, the Earth's nearest star. Inside the Sun, hydrogen atoms fuse together to create helium, releasing vast amounts of energy. This energy travels through space as electromagnetic radiation, including light and infrared (heat) waves. A tiny fraction of this energy reaches the Earth.

The electromagnetic spectrum

The electromagnetic spectrum is the name given to a group of different types of radiation—energy that is given off in the form of waves or rays. Some types of electromagnetic radiation, such as X-rays and ultraviolet light, have more energy than others, such as radio waves. The Sun gives off all types of radiation, but most solar energy that reaches the surface of the Earth is in the form of visible light.

Nature's power plants

Light is essential for life on Earth. Sunlight is absorbed by plants and converted into chemical energy in a process called *photosynthesis*. This energy is passed on to animals when they eat plants or other animals. Animals, including humans, need the energy in food to move and grow.

When infrared radiation hits the Earth, it warms the air, water, and ground. This heat energy keeps the planet warm enough to support life. Solar heat also drives the Earth's weather patterns and the water cycle, the sources of wind, and hydroelectric power (HEP). It was the Sun that powered the growth of millions of plants and animals that decayed to form the world's coal, oil, and gas reserves. When these fossil fuels are burned, the chemical energy locked inside them is changed back into heat and light energy that can be used.

Harnessing the Sun's energy

Humans have found many different ways of using the Sun's energy directly. The Sun's heat and light are used to warm and light buildings, and to generate electricity. Solar energy can even be employed to make hydrogen, used in fuel cells to power vehicles (see page 40). Some people believe that solar power has the potential to meet all of the world's energy needs.

> **" Even if we were to dam every river in the world, and put wind turbines wherever there is wind, it wouldn't be enough to provide for our energy needs. But with solar energy we could meet the world's energy demands. "**
>
> Professor Jacob Karni, Director of Center for Energy Research, Weizmann Institute of Science, Israel

Using heat from the Sun

Heat, or thermal energy, from the Sun has been used by people for thousands of years. Archaeologists believe that the ancient Romans and Greeks designed entire cities to take advantage of solar heat. In 1767, a Swiss scientist built the world's first solar collector, known as a *hot box*, to trap heat from the Sun and cook food. In the 1800s, solar-heated steam engines were used to power factories.

People still use solar heat for many everyday tasks, such as drying clothes. In hot parts of the world, the Sun's energy is often used to improve the quality of food. Fruit, vegetables, fish, meat, and crops can all be dried in the Sun—a useful way to preserve food where refrigeration is not available.

Passive solar heating

Heat from the Sun travels through space as invisible infrared waves. Any object they strike absorbs these waves, and heats up. In sunny conditions, buildings can become very warm. Solar radiation passes through glass windows and warms surfaces inside. The glass stops some of the heat from escaping. Buildings can be designed to increase this effect, known as passive solar heating. Greenhouses are a simple example—solar radiation travels through the glass and some of this energy is changed to heat, which is trapped inside by the glass. Once the greenhouse has been built, the heating source is free.

Solar cooking

Solar heat can also be used to cook food and sterilize water. More than half a million solar stoves are estimated to be in use around the world. Most are found in rural areas of LEDCs, where electricity may not be available and fuel is expensive or difficult to collect. Solar stoves have great potential in countries such as India, which are sunny for more than six months of the year. However, people need training to set up and use solar stoves, and they can be reluctant to change their cooking habits and customs. Solar stoves do not get as hot as wood or charcoal fires, so cooking takes longer.

Active solar heating

Special solar collectors can be placed on the roof of a building to absorb infrared radiation. They heat air or water and circulate it around the building. This is known as *active solar heating*. Enormous versions of these collectors can accumulate enough heat energy to boil water, make steam, and turn an electricity generator.

THE ARGUMENT: Solar heating should be developed further

For:
- Creates no air pollution.
- Solar heat is available all over the world and is free.
- Can be used in many different ways, including making electricity.
- Can replace energy-consuming appliances, such as clothes driers.
- Heat can be stored and released slowly at night.

Against:
- Active solar heating requires costly equipment.
- Heat varies according to location and the time of day and year.
- Equipment will not work at night, or in cloudy conditions.

△ A solar stove being used in the Indian Himalayas.

CASE STUDY:
Solar stoves in India

Bysanivaripalle, a small village in Northern India, has 26 solar stoves. A large, curved mirror—called a *parabola*—collects the Sun's rays and focuses them onto a small, central oven, which becomes very hot. The stoves are used to boil rice, fry potatoes, roast nuts, and make traditional sweets, cakes, and cookies. Even the village ironing is done using heat from the stoves. On a sunny day, water can be heated to 212°F (100°C), killing many disease-causing microbes and making it safe to drink.

Before they received the stoves, the inhabitants of Bysanivaripalle had to rely on collecting and burning firewood. This process is very time-consuming, and leads to local air pollution and health complaints, especially in women who do most of the cooking. The only problem from the stoves is glare from the mirrored surfaces, but the villagers have been given sunglasses to protect their eyes. The village saves enough firewood each year to reduce CO_2 emissions by 113 tons (115 tonnes.)

Using light from the Sun

Sunlight can be turned directly into electricity using photovoltaic cells, also called *solar cells*. In the 1800s, Antoine-Cesar Becquerel discovered that some materials, such as metals, give off electrons when they are exposed to electromagnetic radiation, such as light (see page 8). "Photo" is Greek for light, and electricity is a flow of electrons, so this is known as the *photoelectric effect*.

In 1941, the U.S. scientist Russell Ohl invented the solar cell, to convert sunlight into usable electricity. Photovoltaic (PV) cells are made out of special materials called *semiconductors*. These materials conduct electricity, but not as well as metals. This means that the electricity flowing through a semiconductor can be captured and controlled.

Silicon is the most common semiconductor used to make solar cells. A typical solar cell has two layers of silicon. Different impurities are added to each layer to give them slightly different properties. When light energy strikes the cell, it knocks electrons out of place. These electrons flow between the two layers of silicon, creating an electric current.

▽ How a photovoltaic cell works. When light energy hits a photovoltaic cell, it causes electrons to move from one silicon layer to the other and flow out around the circuit.

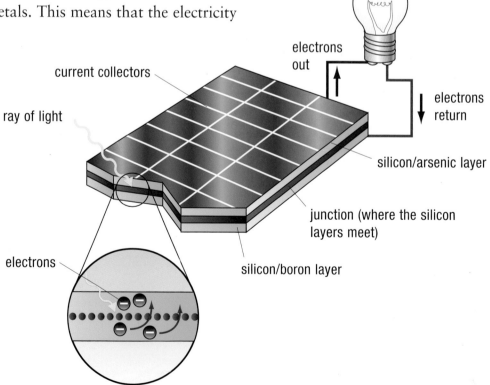

electrons out

electrons return

current collectors

ray of light

silicon/arsenic layer

junction (where the silicon layers meet)

electrons

silicon/boron layer

Metal contacts on the top and bottom of the cell draw off the current, so it can be used as a source of power.

Different wavelengths

Sunlight is made up of different types of electromagnetic radiation—but silicon can absorb only a certain part of sunlight. Some types of radiation pass straight through; other types knock electrons out of place, but their extra energy is wasted. Even more light energy is wasted when it is reflected by the shiny surface of the solar cell, or changed into heat energy as the cell warms up. In addition, solar cells produce a different type of current from that used in homes and offices, so it must be passed through an inverter to convert it.

Panels and arrays

Photovoltaic technology has been used in space for many years, and it is also familiar as a source of power for calculators. The solar industry is now working to make it cheap and reliable enough to be used on a larger scale. A single solar cell produces only enough power to run a small clock. Solar cells must be linked together in panels to produce larger electrical currents. A solar array is made up of many solar panels. The more cells, the more electricity can be generated—up to several million watts. A million watts is known as a *megawatt* (MW).

Electricity supply is usually measured in units known as kilowatt hours (kW). One kW is equivalent to the energy used by a 100-watt light bulb burning consistently for ten hours.

THE ARGUMENT: Solar cells are a good way to generate electricity

For:
- Sunlight is available worldwide.
- Sunlight is free.
- Solar cells are made as small modules, so they can be used on a small or large scale.

Against:
- Solar cells can use only part of the Sun's energy.
- Sunlight is dispersed over a wide area, not concentrated, so its energy is not focused in one place.
- Cells cannot generate electricity at night, nor can they store sunlight.
- Energy is wasted as heat when the solar cells warm up.
- Solar cells produce direct current electricity, which has to be converted into alternating current to be used in buildings.

CHAPTER 3 · Harnessing solar power

The easiest way of using solar energy is to design buildings that keep themselves at a comfortable temperature by trapping the Sun's heat as it is required. Living areas are positioned toward the Sun, and construction materials chosen to absorb or reflect infrared radiation.

Green buildings

In cool climates in the northern hemisphere, large windows on south-facing walls allow solar radiation to flood in. A "thermal mass," such as a concrete floor, absorbs the energy and releases it slowly, keeping the building warm at night. Double-glazed windows and insulating material in walls and the roof stop trapped heat from escaping. The "green" building design reduces the need for heating systems, so it has the potential to save huge amounts of energy. In the United States, heat lost through windows costs more than $20 billion every year.

▽ These houses in Stockholm, Sweden, are designed to maximize passive solar heating, to cut down on energy use from fossil fuels.

Passive solar design also makes the most of light from the Sun. "Sun pipes" bring more sunlight into rooms using mirrors or fiber optics. The huge supermarket chain, Walmart, is experimenting with natural lighting devices. Many people prefer sunlight to artificial light, so it could make staff and customers happier. It would also save up to 300,000 kW of electricity per store, every year—the amount used by 100 typical homes.

Active solar heating

Solar collectors that heat a building's rooms and water are the most widely used type of solar energy. A basic collector is an insulated box with a glass or plastic cover, and a dark-colored absorber plate. The plate heats up as solar radiation hits it, and transfers the heat to a fluid (air, water, or oil) inside the collector. The fluid is pumped or fanned around the building, or passed to the home hot water supply. A 53–65 sq ft. (5–6 sq m) collector can produce 60 gallons (225 liters) of warm water every day.

Thermal collectors are very popular in Japan and China. In Tokyo, 1.5 million buildings have solar water heaters. In the United States, they are often used to heat swimming pools. In Germany, 4 percent of homes use solar thermal energy, and 95,000 new systems were installed in 2005.

THE ARGUMENT:
Solar thermal systems are a good choice for heating homes

For:
- Few moving parts, so little maintenance is needed.
- Systems last for many years.
- No running costs—the Sun's radiation is free.
- No pollution.
- Reduces use of energy from fossil fuels, lowering energy bills and greenhouse gas emissions.
- Large storage tanks can keep water hot, so it can be used at night.

Against:
- Hot water production peaks in the middle of the day—in a small system, heat is lost if you do not use the water quickly.
- Can be expensive to install, especially in older buildings.
- Electricity is still needed to power appliances, and as a backup heating source.
- Not a reliable source of hot water in cloudy or cold climates.
- In liquid systems, the collector fluid can freeze in cold weather.
- Overheating can be a problem in the summer.

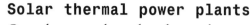

Solar thermal power plants

On a large scale, solar thermal energy can also be used to generate electricity. The Sun's energy is spread over a large area. Solar thermal power plants solve this problem by concentrating the Sun's rays to produce enough heat to drive an electricity generator. This is known as *concentrating solar power*, or CSP. The electricity produced can be fed into the power grid. The grid is the system of power plants, electricity lines, and transformers that deliver electricity to buildings. Electricity from any source can be fed in and distributed around a country.

◁ The mirrors on these solar dishes in Australia focus the Sun's infrared radiation to heat the tubes in the center. These, in turn, transfer the energy to a generator.

How does CSP work?

Mirrors and other optical devices are used to focus solar radiation onto a receiver, which becomes extremely hot. Large concentrating solar power plants can create temperatures of over 1,830°F (1,000°C)—as much as conventional fossil fuel power plants. There are several forms of solar thermal technology, each using lenses or mirrors in different ways.

Solar troughs

Solar troughs are U-shaped glass collectors that focus solar radiation onto steel or glass pipes. Fluid in the pipes heats up and is pumped into heat exchangers, where it boils water to make superheated steam. A steam turbine then generates electricity. Nine power plants using solar troughs have been built in California's Mojave desert since 1991, providing a total of 350 MW of power. Israel has approved plans to build a new 100-MW solar trough plant in the Negev desert. Solar troughs are the least expensive type of solar thermal technology.

Solar towers

Solar towers use large mirrors that track the path of the Sun during the day and focus its rays on a single, big receiver. The solar tower is filled with a fluid, such as molten salt. The fluid is used to produce superheated steam in order to generate electricity.

As the solar energy is concentrated, temperatures of up to 2,700°F (1,500°C) can be generated.

Solar dishes

Solar dishes work like enormous solar stoves, focusing the Sun's rays on a central "hot spot." The heat energy is used to heat metal cylinders, which are filled with hydrogen or helium gas. As the gas expands, it directly drives pistons connected to a generator. Stirling Energy Systems is using this technology to build the world's largest solar thermal farm in the Mojave desert, California—20,000 giant mirrored dishes, arranged in lines miles long, will track the Sun throughout the day. The plant will start feeding 500 MW of electricity into the grid by 2010—as much as a typical fossil fuel plant. This is enough to power 278,000 Californian homes.

> **" [The Stirling] facility will be capable of producing more electricity from solar energy than all U.S. solar projects currently in existence combined. "**
>
> Gil Alexander, Southern California Edison

Small-scale photovoltaics

Solar cells can be linked together in panels and arrays of any size, so they can be used to power everything from a watch to an electricity generator. They are ideal for places where it would be difficult to build electricity cables, such as powering warning buoys at sea, or lights for public telephones in remote areas.

New photovoltaic materials are compact enough to be built into fabric. Soldiers often carry more than 48 pounds (22 kilos) of electrical equipment, including phones, computers, night-vision goggles, and

△ Solar-powered vehicles look impressive, but are not yet practical for everyday use.

batteries to power them. Researchers are developing pocket rechargers, tents embedded with solar panels, and light-sensitive backpacks that will allow soldiers to stay on missions for longer. This technology is also appearing in stores, in the form of bags that can charge telephones and MP3 players.

Solar-powered transportation?

Fossil fuels are popular energy sources, because they can be used in so many ways. Oil can be burned to heat water in an electricity generator, or turned into fuels that power vehicles. With more than 800 million cars on the world's roads, there is great interest in finding an alternative, sustainable, and clean source of energy to power them. Cars powered by solar panels are designed every year, and raced at events such as SunRace Australia. However, they are not as powerful as cars that have a combustion engine, and they are very expensive to make. The solar cells on a single car can cost up to $500,000. A better idea may be electric cars that use batteries charged by stand-alone solar panels, or run on fuel cells powered by solar-generated hydrogen (see page 40).

Solar flight

Aircraft burn a vast amount of fossil fuel, and are responsible for 3.5 percent of global carbon emissions. Almost 2 billion air journeys are made every year, and this increases by 5 percent annually. Some prototype solar-powered aircraft have been designed. In 1981, the Solar Challenger flew across the English Channel, and in 2001, an unmanned solar-powered wing designed by NASA reached a height of almost 19 miles (30 km). Potential uses of super-light craft could include unmanned military surveillance and weather monitoring. It will probably never be possible to build passenger airplanes powered entirely by solar panels, because they would be too heavy and could not fly at night. But eye-catching solar aircraft are a good means of demonstrating the potential of solar technology, since they attract media attention.

THE ARGUMENT:
It is worth developing cars powered by photovoltaic cells

For:
- No polluting fumes.
- Solar panels could be built on the car itself, or used in a separate unit to charge the car's batteries.
- Once the car is bought, the "fuel" that powers it is free.
- Sunlight is available all over the world and will not run out.

Against:
- Electric engines will never be as fast as combustion engines.
- They are expensive to make.
- They would not work at night, and are unreliable on cloudy days.
- Solar cars have to be very small and lightweight.
- There are already so many cars that it would be better to find a way to make existing ones more environmentally friendly.

Photovoltaic power plants

Photovoltaic technology can be used to produce electricity on a large enough scale to feed it into the power grid. PV power stations, also known as *solar farms*, are massive arrays of millions of PV cells. They have been built in several countries, including Japan, Saudi Arabia, the United States, and Germany. One of the largest solar farms is in Leipzig, Germany, where 33,500 solar panels generate up to 5 MW of power on a cloudless day —enough to provide electricity to 1,800 German homes.

Solar farms can be very expensive to set up, but once they are built, they have few moving parts to maintain, and "fuel" is free, meaning they are very reliable sources of power. Unlike HEP plants, solar farms can be built anywhere in the world. Another big advantage is that fuel does not have to be transported to them, as it does to a fossil fuel or biomass power plant.

PV power to Portugal

The world's largest PV plant is being built in Portugal by General Electric Company's Energy Financial Services. It will supply 11 MW—enough to power about 8,000 local homes. A large concentrating solar power (CSP) plant can supply 500 MW (see page 17), and some nuclear, coal, and oil-powered plants produce more than 2,000 MW. But even though it is small

▽ A PV plant in Bakersfield, California. Panels are mounted on a tracking device that aims them at the Sun as it moves across the sky.

in comparison, this Portuguese PV project will reduce greenhouse gases by around 29,000 tons (30,000 tonnes) every year.

Efficiency limits

Not all of the solar energy that reaches a photovoltaic cell can be converted into electricity. The difference between the energy put in and the amount of useful energy produced is determined by the efficiency of the system. Commercial silicon photovoltaic panels are about 15–20 percent efficient. This means that they can convert only 15–20 percent of the energy in sunlight to electrical energy.

The silicon itself is the problem. As we saw on page 13, it can absorb only a certain part of the Sun's light. One answer is to stick different semiconductors together in layers to capture a wider range of light energy—from infrared to ultraviolet. The most efficient combination uses germanium, gallium, and indium. The cells capture 36 percent of the Sun's energy, but they are difficult and costly to make, and use toxic chemicals.

Concentrated PV power

Concentrating solar power (CSP) plants are around 30 percent efficient, and seem more likely to become the first large-scale solar electricity producers. Some PV companies have developed systems that use mirrors or lenses to concentrate the Sun's light up to 500 times, just as thermal energy is concentrated by CSP. This could increase efficiency by up to 50 percent, meaning smaller, cheaper plants could produce the same amount of electricity. However, the cells have to be continuously cooled to prevent overheating, and they will not work in cloudy conditions. Unlike solar heat, sunlight cannot be stored. Small PV systems that can be fixed to roofs may have more long-term potential.

THE ARGUMENT: PV power stations have a future

For:
- Energy source is free.
- They are nonpolluting.
- The technology is reliable because there are few moving parts.
- PV cells can be used anywhere there is sunlight.

Against:
- Very expensive to set up.
- Cover large areas of land.
- Output falls on cloudy days and stops at night.
- Efficiency is limited.

Local power

Converting the chemical energy in coal into electricity, carrying it to homes through the grid, and changing it into light in a conventional light bulb is only 3 percent efficient—97 percent of the original energy in the coal is wasted. Photovoltaic systems have a big advantage—electricity can be produced at the site where it is used, cutting out the need for transmission altogether. This makes the technology ideal for remote locations without a connection to the grid.

Plugging into the Sun

Some homes and businesses that are connected to the grid have also installed their own PV panels to provide electricity. This is known as *microgeneration*, or distributed generation. Most personal PV systems provide enough power to reduce a building's energy bills. The electricity grid, batteries, or a generator, supplies backup power at night and on cloudy days when PV cells have a low output.

PV systems are expensive, and the first grid-connected customers bought them to help reduce carbon emissions rather than to save money. However, the cost has fallen by an average of 4 percent per year since the 1970s, and microgeneration is starting to attract customers who are worried about the uncertain price of fossil fuels. Buying a PV system is equivalent to buying 25–30 years' electricity in advance, so the price per kilowatt hour will stay fixed for that length of time. From 2001 to 2004, the number of grid-connected solar systems grew by 60 percent each year. Many large multinational companies have also installed solar power systems. In 2005, FedEx covered the roof of their huge California depot with over 80,700 square feet (7,500 square meters) of PV panels, which now provide 80 percent of the facility's electricity.

> "I like the idea that we are our own power station. Around two-thirds of our electricity is supplied by solar and wind power, and solar is the main component. Most importantly for me, there are no emissions. It's clean, silent, renewable energy."
>
> David Merrill, Glastonbury, England

Efficiency savings

Becoming more energy efficient by reducing unnecessary power use allows a house to buy a smaller, cheaper PV system. For example, if everyone in the

United States improved their home insulation, used energy-efficient light bulbs and unplugged appliances when not in use, energy demand would fall by up to 20 percent. Net metering (see page 38) also makes solar panels more worthwhile, by allowing customers to sell their spare electricity back to the grid on sunny days.

Energy-balanced homes

The ultimate aim is to set up "zero-energy" homes that feed surplus power into the grid in the summer and draw on the grid in the winter or on cloudy days. Overall, they produce at least as much energy from solar panels as they use each year. The U.S. Department of Energy's Building America program has built more than 26,000 homes as research projects. They blend energy-efficient strategies with other forms of renewable energy, such as thermal heaters. The latest combinations of PV and solar thermal roofing tiles can generate hot water and electricity, even on cloudy days. At the moment, a zero-energy home costs 10–20 percent more to build than a traditional home. Although this is "paid back" in energy savings over 20–30 years, buyers are put off by the higher upfront cost. The challenge is to make solar-powered homes cheaper.

▽ Solar power is ideal for use in remote locations. It is much easier for this hiker to carry a small solar panel than fuel or batteries.

CHAPTER 4 The environment and resources

Solar thermal and photovoltaic systems can be installed almost anywhere, and on any scale—from heat collectors on a house, to fields of solar cells. However, due to varied climatic conditions, their productivity differs greatly around the world.

The right conditions

Thermal mirror collectors are efficient only in sunny areas free of mist and smog. The Sun's rays are strongest at the equator, around the middle of the Earth, but most areas near the equator also have a high annual rainfall and therefore regular cloud cover. Solar power is most effective in places near the equator that also have clear skies year-round, such as deserts.

▽ PV panels do work in cloudy climates, but their electricity output falls. More panels are needed to generate the same amount of power as cells located in sunny conditions.

> **"** Solar radiation patterns around the globe are our most reliable and predictable resource. **"**
>
> Tim Townsend, alternative energy specialist based in Davis, California

Transmission problems

Desert regions have large areas of unused land available for building solar power plants, but they are not comfortable areas to live in. It would also be difficult and expensive to build transmission lines to carry electricity from big desert power stations to the towns and cities where it is needed. When electricity is transmitted through the grid, energy is wasted due to resistance in the wires that carry it. More than 7 percent of the energy generated is lost in this way. Solar panels on rooftops are more efficient, because they generate electricity at the place where it is used.

Weather patterns

Less solar energy reaches the ground in cloudy areas far from the equator, because solar radiation has to pass through a greater amount of atmosphere. Washington state, for example, receives about 40 percent less sunshine than "hot spots" in the southern states that make up the Sunbelt. The less sunny an area, the more PV panels must be installed to generate a certain amount of electricity. Newer solar cells that use thin films of different semiconductors promise to improve electricity production in lower light conditions, but they are currently very expensive to make. Mounting solar panels on a tracking device, which aims them directly at the Sun as it moves across the sky, can increase power output.

The average daily temperature is an important factor, too. Silicon cells produce less electricity the hotter they become. They work best in cold regions with clear skies, or in areas with cooling winds. PV panels located on a high, cool, and sunny mountain slope will perform better than those located in a warmer desert.

> **"** In the cloudy United Kingdom, we can provide more electricity than the country currently uses just with solar PV on existing rooftops. **"**
>
> Jeremy Leggett, Chief Executive of Solarcentury, a PV solar consultancy, U.K.

Land use

A vast amount of solar energy reaches the Earth every day, but it is dispersed across a wide area. This means large areas of solar panels are needed to collect it. Even in a very sunny place, a PV plant that could power a town would have to be larger than the town itself. The solar power facility at Kramer Junction, California, consists

△ Architects are finding creative ways to incorporate solar panels into the design of buildings, such as this apartment building in Los Angeles, California.

of five generating stations with a combined output of 150 MW. This is enough power for about 150,000 local homes. The plant covers over 43 million sq ft. (4 million sq m).

It has been estimated that it would take around 38,600 sq mi. (100,000 sq km) of solar panels to meet the United States' electricity needs. However, solar panels do not have to be placed on open land. Roofs, walls, and "useless" land at roadsides can be turned into solar farms. One of the largest photovoltaic solar power systems in the United States has been built on the roof of the Santa Rita Jail in California, where 129,000 square feet (12,000 square meters) of solar panels generate 1.18 MW—30 percent of the electricity used by the jail.

CASE STUDY: Rooftop solar

Land near towns and cities is expensive, adding to the price of solar power plants. A company called Sun Edison has avoided this problem with a clever scheme. It installs grid-connected solar panels on the roofs of stores for free, and sells the power back to them at a fixed price. The stores are protected against future electricity price rises, but do not have to run and maintain the solar panels themselves. Whole Foods, for example, has panels installed in several of its stores, and now saves 11 percent annually on electricity bills. Customers are also attracted to stores that seem "green."

The problem of shade

Building solar plants on rooftops and walls would also bring the electricity supply closer to the source of demand, cutting down on transmission waste. However, it involves another problem —shade. Most solar panels are made of crystalline silicon. If just one cell is shaded, it blocks the flow of electricity between all the cells in that section. A shadow covering just 3 percent of the panel halves the power output. Solar panels on rooftops and walls would have to be carefully placed to avoid shading from nearby buildings. Trees that blocked sunlight would have to be cut down. Cells that use amorphous silicon cope better with high temperatures and shading. But they are bulkier and less efficient, and some people dislike their appearance.

Integrated design

PV panels can be made in different colors to blend in with brickwork or tiles, or built into the roof or walls of a building so they are not immediately visible. This is known as *building-integrated photovoltaics*, and is more expensive than installing freestanding units. It is more often used in new office buildings than in homes.

Environmental hazards

The term *renewable* refers to energy sources that can be sustained forever, either because the supply is constant (like the Sun) or because it renews itself (like biomass). Many people associate the word *renewable* with "green"—but all energy sources have an impact on the environment. It is important for energy planning to balance environmental impact with the amount of useful energy produced. Once a solar thermal or photovoltaic system is installed, there are no greenhouse gas emissions. Systems do not cause noise pollution and the energy source, solar radiation, is free and completely renewable. However, the production of solar cells and other solar energy systems is not as environmentally friendly.

Making solar panels

Solar panels are made in four stages. Lumps of pure silicon are melted at temperatures of 2,912°F (1,600°C), and cooled to produce silicon crystal wafers. The wafers are then processed to make working solar cells. Next, cells are soldered together to make modules, and sandwiched between a sheet of glass and an aluminum frame. Finally, the solar modules are assembled into a solar system, such as a roof panel. This stage involves wiring the panel into the electricity supply of a building or appliance, and sometimes into the grid. Each stage usually takes place at a different plant, so more energy is used in transportation between sites. At the moment, most factories are powered by energy from fossil fuels.

CASE STUDY: Solar heaters in Scandinavia

Solar water heaters generally have a shorter payback time than PV panels—around one to two years. In Ballerup, Denmark, six solar collectors provide hot water for 100 families. Because the storage tanks are so large, they can keep water hot for weeks at a time. Using the solar heater along with other energy-saving measures, such as insulation, has cut bills by 60 percent—and fossil fuel use has declined so carbon emissions are reduced. However, solar heaters can only heat water; they cannot make electricity. An electricity supply is needed too, and often a backup source of heating in the winter. At the moment, this usually comes from burning fossil fuels. One solution is to use PV panels combined with active solar heating.

This means that a certain amount of carbon is released into the atmosphere for every solar panel made. It takes a few years for the energy produced from each manufactured solar panel to balance the energy used in its production. This time is known as the *energy payback*. It is the time taken to "pay back" the carbon emissions from the manufacturing process.

Energy payback

It is difficult to calculate the energy payback time of a home or office PV system. It depends on the amount of sunshine, the size and type of system, and whether it can feed spare electricity into the grid. The average estimate is four years. PV cells last for 25–30 years, so they would repay their energy input seven times over their lifetime. Technological advances promise to reduce this payback time. Larger solar farms may have a payback time of 20 years or longer, because more energy is used to build facilities and transmission lines.

▽ Creating PV panels is complex. The panels have to be used for an average of four years before they have "paid back" the electrical energy used to make them.

Raw materials

The cost of photovoltaic systems has fallen by around 4 percent a year for the past 15 years. Cells are becoming more efficient, so fewer cells are needed to produce a given amount of power, and demand has risen, so they are manufactured on a larger scale. However, the high demand has given the PV industry a new problem.

Around 90 percent of solar cells are made from crystalline silicon, the same material used to make computer chips. There is plenty of silicon in the Earth's crust, but the main sources—sand and quartz—are not pure. They contain metal atoms, which attract electrons and reduce the solar cell's efficiency.

▽ Purified silicon is in high demand, due to rapid growth in electronics and PV industries.

Purifying silicon is expensive and time-consuming, and uses lots of energy. It means that solar cell makers have to pay more for their raw material, and it increases the energy payback time. Silicon prices are expected to rise dramatically in the next few years, so manufacturers are searching for economical alternatives.

Solar cells for the future

Solar panel producers are designing cells that use less silicon. Others are exploring nonsilicon technology, especially panels that use thin films of semiconducting materials. CIGS cells, a sandwich of thin films of copper, indium, and gallium selenide, use 99 percent less raw material than silicon cells. CIGS cells are cheaper to make and can be layered straight onto glass or steel sheets, cutting out a stage

in the manufacturing process and saving energy. Shell's solar division is currently developing a film that could halve the price of solar panels by 2012. However, the average thin-film solar module is just 6 percent efficient at the moment.

Reducing waste

The most environmentally friendly solution is to design buildings for passive solar heating and lighting. This can meet up to 90 percent of the heating needs of a building without requiring any power generation. Reducing energy use by half is just as good for the Earth as providing half your energy needs with a solar thermal or PV system, and is much cheaper.

▽ Thin-film PV cells use much less raw material than silicon cells but are less efficient.

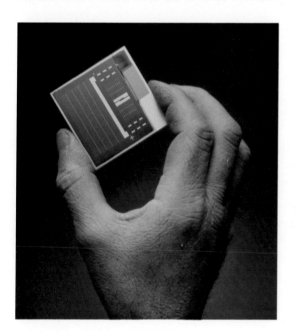

THE ARGUMENT: Photovoltaic cells are environmentally friendly

For:

- No greenhouse gas emissions.
- Solar radiation is completely renewable.
- Unlike wind turbines, PV cells are silent.
- Small systems save the energy used to make them in around four years.
- Silicon is the second most abundant element in the Earth's crust.

Against:

- Silicon purification and panel production requires energy, which currently comes from burning nonrenewable fossil fuels.
- Alternative solar cells are made with toxic chemicals.
- Plastic cells have a short lifetime, creating waste.
- The most affordable and efficient panels are bulky and can look ugly.
- Large systems may take 20 years or more to pay back the energy used to make them.

Reliability

The main disadvantage of solar power is that the Sun's energy reaches the ground only during the day. Homes with solar systems need backup power from batteries, the grid, or a private generator at night.

Batteries

Batteries are expensive, bulky, waste some of the electricity produced, and are harder to maintain than a PV system itself. They contain dangerous chemicals and have to be kept in a special enclosure, which adds to the cost of installation. They also need replacing every five years, and harm the environment if they are not disposed of carefully. However, they are useful in remote areas that are far from a mainstream grid.

Net metering

Decentralized photovoltaic systems can "store" solar electricity by selling any surplus back to the grid, usually in the middle of the day. They can then use the grid for backup power at night and on cloudy days. This is called *net metering*, and it makes PV systems more affordable. Solar panels also work well if they are integrated

▽ PV panels can be combined with wind power to produce a reliable electricity supply in most weather, as at the Ecotech Centre, Norfolk, U.K.

with a wind turbine. This provides important backup power at times when the Sun is not shining.

Power plants

Unlike light energy, thermal energy can be stored—just as a drink stays hot in a thermos bottle. By storing the Sun's heat, solar thermal power plants can keep generating electricity after dark. These power plants are more likely than PV farms to become the first large producers of solar electricity.

CASE STUDY: Solar Two

Solar One and Solar Two are the most famous prototype large-scale concentrating solar power plants. Solar One was built in California in 1982, and upgraded to Solar Two in 1996. It uses hundreds of mirrors to focus the Sun's radiation at a central tower, where molten salt flows through stainless steel tubes. The tubes are painted black to absorb 95 percent of the sunlight reflected at them. The absorbed heat energy is stored in the salt at 1,050°F (565°C), so it can drive turbines and generate electricity 24 hours a day. Spain is now building an 11-MW solar tower plant, and two more 20-MW towers are planned.

THE ARGUMENT: Private, on-site PV panels are a good option

For:
- They reduce the need to build or upgrade distribution networks.
- Low ongoing costs, because there are no moving parts to maintain.
- Small modules are unlikely to fail all at once, so blackouts are rare.
- Surplus power can be "stored" by feeding it into the grid for credit.
- Costs do not vary with the price of fossil fuels.
- Technology is very reliable—panels last for around 25 years.
- Cuts down on energy wasted by transmission through the grid.
- Highest output is during the middle of the day—a peak time for office buildings—when grid electricity is expensive.

Against:
- Power supply is interrupted at night and in cloudy weather.
- Not very efficient in cloudy climates.
- Needs backup supply from the grid, a generator, or batteries.
- Big upfront costs.
- Lowest output is in winter, a time of high electricity demand.

CHAPTER 5   Cost and investment

The Sun's energy may be free, but the technology needed to convert it into a usable form is expensive. A fossil fuel-burning power plant can produce electricity for about $0.02–0.04 per kilowatt hour. Power from a large photovoltaic plant costs $0.20 or more per kilowatt hour. The high cost of solar power means that it is currently used to generate just 0.06 percent of the world's electricity.

Technology drives demand

Some people believe that demand for solar power will increase only when solar technology becomes cheaper and more efficient. Governments can make a difference by investing directly in research and development.

Jet planes, computers, the Internet, and cell phones were all funded by governments for many years, before they became cheap enough to be considered for general use.

In 2006, the state of California, committed more than $3.35 billion to establishing 3,000 MW of solar power over the next ten years. This is the United States' largest-ever solar program, and it should set a good example for the future.

▽ Vast solar farms like this one in the Mojave Desert are expensive to install, and most of them rely on government backing. They have the potential to generate electricity without pollution.

New ideas and innovation will improve solar technology, but for now, fossil fuels remain a cheaper energy source. However, this ignores the long-term cost to the environment, and the health of populations. Can we afford to wait for solar power to become cheap, while greenhouse gas emissions from fossil fuels continue to damage the world?

Demand drives technology

Some people argue that the priority of governments should be to educate citizens about climate change and the benefits of renewable resources. This would increase the demand for solar power, which would lead to investment and research. Many governments, including those in Italy, Germany, Japan, Spain and states such as California, provide incentives to kick-start demand for solar power by making it more cost-effective.

In the United States, a household solar energy system costs $0.22–0.40 per kilowatt hour. Government subsidies can bring this down to around $0.09–0.11. Germany has spent billions on promoting solar power since 1990, and has an energy tax, used to subsidize renewables. In Spain, all new buildings must include a solar power source. The solar industry has grown rapidly in both Spain and Germany, and Germany is a world leader in solar thermal technology.

CASE STUDY: Chinese investment in solar power

China is the world's second-largest energy user after the United States. The IEA (International Energy Agency) predicts that by 2020, China's greenhouse gas emissions will have doubled. The Chinese government wants to reduce its dependency on coal and oil. In 2005, it pledged to switch 15 percent of China's energy use to renewable sources, and committed the equivalent of $180 billion over the next 15 years to fund this.

PV technology has enormous potential in China. Two-thirds of the land receives more than 2,000 hours of sunlight yearly. If this energy was harnessed by PV panels, it would create as much power as burning 1,840 billion tons (1,870 billion tonnes) of coal per year. Some 29,000 villages—home to 30 million people—are not linked to China's national grid. Under a landmark renewable energy law, Chinese electricity users now pay an extra 0.2 percent for their power. The money is used to supply cheap PV technology to rural areas.

Is solar power economically viable anywhere?

Solar energy is already cost-effective in many remote locations, such as lighthouses, where it would be too expensive to connect to the grid.
In the U.K., for example, more than 1,000 bus shelters and parking meters, in 11 cities are powered by solar energy. This demand is helping to boost research.

Solar power is also being used in some LEDCs. It allows people who live far from power lines to supply their communities with electricity. In three villages in Jigawa state, Nigeria, solar panels drive water pumps, light classrooms, and power local businesses. The local community works together to look after the fragile panels, and says that solar energy has changed people's lives for the better. Photovoltaics would be the cheapest way of providing power for

> **" Solar was the obvious solution. Not only would we be helping economic development, but we would also cut down on deforestation, which is such a big problem here. "**
>
> Mohammad Sani Muhammad, Jigawa Alternative Energy Fund, Nigeria

∇ Solar panels, such as these at a Nigerian school, can greatly improve the quality of life for communities without access to a power grid. Once installed, they provide a free and reliable electricity supply.

1.6 billion people who are currently without electricity in LEDCs. But these people are least able to afford it. At $8,000 per village, Jigawa relied on funding from a U.S. organization, though the state government has funded 30 more schemes.

The spread of solar energy will largely depend on schemes such as the World Bank's Solar Initiative. The Kyoto agreement allows wealthier countries to invest in renewable energy schemes in LEDCs, to compensate for their own carbon emissions.

> " The best course is to allow every method of producing or saving energy to compete fairly, at honest prices, regardless of which kind of investment it is, what technology it uses, how big it is, or who owns it. "
>
> Amory Lovins, co-founder of Rocky Mountain Institute, Colorado

CASE STUDY:
Investment by oil companies

The Kyoto agreement has boosted business interest in solar power. Targets for using renewable energy give the solar industry a guarantee that their technology will be in demand. The global solar industry was worth almost $11.2 billion in 2005, and is expected to grow to $51 billion by 2015.

The oil companies Shell and BP are two of the world's biggest PV technology producers. These companies are keen to appear "green," by using their huge wealth to invest in renewable resources. However, their investment in solar power is still minimal compared to the money spent exploring for oil each year. BP Solar is expected to earn $1.1 billion in 2008. But this is just a tiny fraction of BP's overall revenue of $260 billion.

Most governments also support their fossil fuel industries more than they support renewable energies. The United States, for example, subsidizes gas, making it cheaper than bottled water. If fossil fuel emissions were heavily taxed, people would switch to renewables much more quickly. However, green policies that raise fuel prices like this are very unpopular with industry and voters.

Led by profit

Electricity suppliers buy electricity from power stations and then sell it to the public at a higher price. At the moment, fossil fuel power stations can supply them with much cheaper electricity than renewable sources can. However, the higher price that each household pays for electricity is closer to the cost of installing their own solar panels. Many members of the solar industry believe that microgeneration will become competitive within a few years. Schemes that allow people to borrow money to install PV technology, and pay it off gradually, also help to grow the industry.

> " We're four to five years away from the point at which solar is cost-effective with traditional electricity generation without any subsidy. "
>
> Norm Taffe, Vice President for Cypress Semiconductor's Consumer Division, speaking at Globalpress Summit, Monterey, California, 2006

Plugging into the grid

Net metering is one of the best ways to encourage households to buy their own PV panels. It means they can "plug in" to the grid and sell their spare electricity to utility companies. On a sunny day, each house becomes a minipower plant. Germany's "Feed-in Law" means that people with solar panels are paid $0.55 per kilowatt hour for their electricity. Spain and Italy have similar plans. Most U.S. states allow net metering, but the amount customers are paid for their power is often much lower than the price of conventional power.

Meeting demand

Net metering can make economic sense for electricity companies. Demand for electricity in the United States has grown faster than the companies can supply it. High demand partly caused the August 2003 blackout in North America, which left millions of people without power. It is cheaper to pay customers to produce their own power than to build new power stations and transmission lines. Rooftop solar panels are particularly helpful, because they produce power during the middle of the day—a time of peak electricity demand.

A win-win measure

One important action governments can take is to encourage people to become more efficient energy users. Many politicians and industry leaders believe that protecting the climate will damage our standard of living by increasing the cost of energy—and

everything that uses it. However, energy efficiency does not mean doing less. It means finding ways to do the same things using less energy. It cuts energy bills, reduces greenhouse gas emissions, and makes renewable technologies, such as solar power, more realistic long-term solutions. The cost of a personal solar power system, for example, becomes less if the house uses less energy to start with. Fewer solar panels, or a smaller thermal collector, would be needed if steps were taken to prevent energy wastage.

△ It is easier and cheaper to install solar systems in new buildings than to add them to existing homes and offices.

❝ We ought to be purchasing energy efficiency to save money. If we do it right, the environmental benefit comes free. ❞

Amory Lovins, co-founder of Rocky Mountain Institute

CHAPTER 6

Solar power in the future

Three decades ago, computers were huge and much too expensive for individuals to buy. The Internet had not been invented, and no one owned a cell phone. This shows how, in a short time, new inventions can catch on and spread around the world. Many researchers are striving to find the solar technology of the future that will solve the world's energy crisis.

Thin-film cells

One key aim is to make solar cells that use thin films of semiconducting material more efficient. In 2005, NREL (National Renewable Energy Laboratory) found that plastic studded with microscopic crystals could, in theory, make solar cells that capture 70 percent of the Sun's light energy. Nanotechnology could also make cells work better under weak lighting conditions. PV substances could be printed on surfaces, or woven into fabric, so clothes could generate the electricity to power your cell phone and MP3 player.

Storing electricity

Japanese researchers have created the world's first photocapacitor—a solar cell that creates and stores electricity. Layers of carbon trap electrons and hold them until a switch completes the circuit. If solar panels could store energy like this, they would be able to produce electricity 24 hours a day.

Hydrogen fuel

Hydrogen is a nonpolluting fuel that can be used in a fuel cell to power cars or homes. Some people believe it is the fuel of the future. Electricity from PV cells can be used to split water into hydrogen and oxygen. It currently takes more energy to make hydrogen than the gas gives back as a fuel, but this process would be a good way of converting solar energy into a fuel that can be stored. At the moment, it is ten times cheaper to make hydrogen by reacting steam with natural gas, a fossil fuel. However, as supplies of natural gas run out, solar-generated hydrogen could become competitive.

The Weizmann Institute in Israel uses solar technology to generate hydrogen on a large scale. A solar tower (see page 17) is used to heat zinc oxide to 2,192°F (1,200°C), releasing gaseous zinc, which can be condensed into powder. When zinc reacts with water, it produces hydrogen and zinc oxide. The chemical reaction releases no greenhouse gases, and the zinc oxide can be recycled into pure zinc and used again to repeat the process.

CASE STUDY: Hydrogen buses

The Californian bus company, SunLine, has a fleet of fuel-cell vehicles. Hydrogen is produced at the depot using renewable energy sources, including solar power. Fuel cells make very little noise compared to regular engines, and are less likely to break down. The only emissions are water and air, and because the hydrogen is generated using "clean" power, the buses produce zero pollution. In addition, battery packs on-board store energy as the bus brakes. This helps the vehicles to travel up to three times farther per gallon of fuel than conventional buses.

> **"** There is a chicken-and-egg issue here. Who is going to build a [fuel-cell] car before they have [hydrogen] filling stations, and who is going to build stations before we have the cars? **"**
>
> Dr. David Auty, Chief Executive of Hydrogen Solar, a U.S. and U.K. hydrogen power development company

▽ Some of SunLine's buses run on Hythane® —a blend of hydrogen and natural gas. This is an economical way to start using hydrogen, and it has lower emissions than pure natural gas.

Artificial photosynthesis

During photosynthesis, green plants use the energy in sunlight to split water molecules into oxygen and hydrogen. The energy released is used to convert carbon dioxide to storable chemical energy (in the form of carbohydrates). Technology that copies photosynthesis could be the key to the world's energy problems, producing both hydrogen for fuel cells, and absorbing excess carbon dioxide from the atmosphere. Konarka, whose founder won a Nobel prize for pioneering organic solar cells, is leading research into artificial photosynthesis.

> **"** Photosynthesis is the most successful solar converting mechanism on Earth. And when nature has invented such a successful system, it would be foolish to ignore it as a potential source of renewable energy. **"**
>
> Stenbjorn Styring, Professor of Biochemistry at Lund University, Sweden

▽ There is a huge potential for harnessing solar energy in space. The Mars Rovers are exploratory robots, powered by solar panels. They have survived the Martian winter and dust storms, and are celebrated as symbols of how reliable and durable solar power can be.

Solar power from space

Solar power is already used to power satellites and other space vehicles. The next step is to design systems that could power long-distance space flight, which would be much safer than using nuclear power. Researchers at the University of California envisage giant solar panels that are unrolled like carpets to soak up the Sun's energy.

An even more ambitious idea is to generate solar power in space, where there are no clouds, and beam it down to Earth. In 2001, the Japanese Space Agency NASDA announced plans to develop a satellite-based solar power system that beams energy back to Earth via an airship. The Moon is the ultimate satellite—some researchers believe that one day we could generate solar power on the Moon and beam it back to Earth as microwaves.

A solar future?

Reading an impressive list of innovative solar technology research, it is possible to imagine a totally solar-powered future. All buildings would feature energy-efficient design, construction and materials, and produce their own heat and electricity from thermal collectors and panels of solar cells. Breakthroughs in PV materials and cell designs would see cars, planes, and even clothes produce safe, clean, electric power. Solar electricity would be used to produce hydrogen for fuel cells, powering vehicles as well as buildings.

In reality, solar will be one part of an overall energy mix, along with nuclear power, the remaining fossil fuels, and other renewable energy resources. The significance of solar power in this mix will depend on both government help and technological progress.

THE ARGUMENT: Ambitious solar projects should be encouraged

For:
- Unique ideas can capture investors' imagination and boost research.
- A wider range of technology means a wider range of solutions for different parts of the world.
- It makes sense to experiment with new and innovative ways of using Earth's vast solar energy reserves.

Against:
- Limited investment funds could be directed at more realistic ideas.
- Practical and technological difficulties are extensive.
- Failure of a big project in the public eye could cause doubt about other types of renewable energy.

Solar potential

Rising energy bills, climate concern, fears about energy security, and improved technology are all increasing demand for renewable power. Solar power is environmentally friendly, available everywhere, and versatile. It is also, currently, the most expensive form of renewable energy—but costs are coming down and the energy source itself is free. In 2005, global production of PV cells jumped by 45 percent to almost 1,730 MW—six times the level in 2000. With increased efficiency, or a continued rise in overall energy prices, rooftop solar panels might become competitive with conventional power in a few years. In many remote areas, solar panels are already the cheapest and most efficient way to generate electricity. Designing or improving buildings to benefit from passive solar heating and lighting is also cost-effective already.

> **The technology works. It's reliable, it's efficient. The question is, how do you make the leap in scale, in terms of manufacturing?**
>
> Thomas R Mancini, Manager of the Solar Power Program at Sandia National Labs, Livermore, California

Solar power is economical only on a small scale at the moment, but concentrating solar power (CSP) is expected to be as cheap as conventional power within a decade, due to advances in technology. CSP has the potential to harness enough of the Sun's energy to provide electricity on a massive scale. In the southwestern states, for example, a desert area of 150 square miles (388 square kilometers) could provide 20,000 MW of power. Government initiatives will be essential to make this a reality.

Short-term change for long-term effect

The easiest way to tackle carbon emissions is to use energy more efficiently. This will also make solar power more viable in the long term. Preventable energy waste costs the world more than $1 trillion every year. About 5 percent of U.S. and 7 percent of U.K. domestic electricity use is lost to appliances on standby. This is damaging the environment while providing no value. Many cheap, energy-efficient products are available, but people either do not know about them, or are unaware of how important it is to use them.

Little has been done to boost energy efficiency so far. In many countries, taxpayer-funded subsidies have made energy seem cheap. Habits, such as leaving cell phone chargers plugged in, and leaving lights on, are hard to change. Governments need to educate the public about the environmental and economic benefits of using less energy. MEDCs also need to help LEDCs, by sharing the technology needed to use energy efficiently. Energy savings would help to speed development by releasing money to fund essential services, such as education and healthcare.

"I believe that solar energy will be the future energy resource for human beings, and that by the middle of this century it will account for 20–30 percent of energy generation. "

Nicoletta Marigo, the Environmental Policy and Management Group, Imperial College London, U.K.

▽ Every year the U.S. Department of Energy challenges students to design homes that can generate enough renewable energy to meet the average family's needs.

Glossary

Active solar heating The heating of a building or object by special devices designed to trap solar heat.

Array A large number of solar panels grouped together.

Biomass Any plant or animal material. It can be used as a source of energy.

Electromagnetic radiation Energy in the form of waves or rays, such as light or heat.

Electron A tiny, charged particle that orbits the center of an atom.

Fossil fuels The coal, oil, and natural gas that come from the remains of ancient plants and animals.

Fuel cell A device that converts chemical energy in a fuel directly to electrical energy without burning.

Global warming The rise in average temperature of the Earth's surface due to an increased greenhouse effect.

Greenhouse effect Warming of the Earth's climate due to gases in the atmosphere that trap solar heat before it can be radiated back into space.

Greenhouse gases Atmospheric gases that cause the greenhouse effect.

Microgeneration Producing electricity on a small scale at the site where it is used—also known as *distributed generation*.

Nanotechnology A science that works with materials on a microscopic scale.

Parabola A U-shaped mirror or dish, designed to focus solar radiation.

Passive solar heating Direct heating of a building or object by the Sun's rays.

Photosynthesis The process by which plants use light energy to convert carbon dioxide from the air into carbohydrates, which are stored and used by the plant as food.

Photovoltaic (PV) cell A device, made of layers of semiconducting material, that produces a small electric current when it absorbs light energy.

Renewable Something that can be sustained forever, either because it will never run out, or because it can be replanted.

Semiconductor A material such as silicon that conducts electricity, but not as well as a conductor such as metal (used in electrical wiring).

Solar collector A panel or other device that absorbs infrared radiation from the Sun.

Sustainable Can be maintained without depleting a natural resource.

Turbine A machine in which a gas or liquid turns blades to produce movement energy that can be converted to electrical energy.

Books to read

Looking At Energy: Solar Power Polly Goodman, Wayland, London, 2005: explains all about solar power, past, present, and future.

Planet Under Pressure: Energy Clive Gifford, Heinemann Library, London, 2006: an excellent summary of the energy crisis facing the world.

Solar Power of the Future: New Ways of Turning Sunlight into Energy Susan Jones, Rosen Publishing Group, New York, 2004: contains a detailed history of solar power and the new technologies being developed for the future.

Solar Power (True Book Series) Christine Petersen, Children's Press, Danbury, 2004: a look at the place of solar power in today's society.

Web Sites

Due to the changing nature of Internet links, The Rosen Publishing Group, Inc., has developed an online list of Web sites related to the subject of this book. This site is updated regularly. Please use this link to access the list:
www.rosenlinks.com/ted/solar/

Index

Note: Page numbers in *italic* refer to illustrations.